INTO THE FLAMES

WRITTEN BY

ROBERT L. RITCHEY
AND
SANDI L. (RITCHEY) HILDERMAN

ISBN 978-1-63961-173-7 (paperback)
ISBN 978-1-63961-174-4 (digital)

Christian Faith Publishing, Inc.
832 Park Avenue
Meadville, PA 16335
www.christianfaithpublishing.com

Printed in the United States of America

I dedicate this book in loving memory to my brother, Robert L. Ritchey. He lived it, he wrote about it, then passed away years after it should have been published. I also dedicate this book to the Wildland firefighters and the Forest Service for their commitment to a dangerous job. Your family and friends love you and miss you, Bob. But we know we will see you again!

Your sis, San

GLACIER PARK

Wrong Creek Cabin Fire

That was great! They flew us plus equipment in by choppers and dropped us off. Still don't know where I was—somewhere in the middle of nowhere in Glacier Park Forest. No way in or out except by chopper. Alas, the cabin was burnt up. Every day, morning and evening, hot meals were brought in by chopper for us.

Days were warm, evenings and mornings were fricking cold. It rained a couple of days and soaked everything—

tents, gear, etc. The fun was gone after the second week when it snowed on us. The choppers couldn't see to land, let alone even get to us. We found ourselves all alone in timber and no way out...and nothing but MREs to eat (Meals Ready to Eat) three times a day. We had gotten soaked and then snowed on, and now no supplies, including hot food.

We kept the campfires going and tried to dry clothing and other stuff out. Some of us already had colds. Three days in a row, our crew boss was told they'd try and get a chopper in to us.

"Can't fly today!"

"Weather!"

Finally, at 0700, we got the call: "Pack up and be ready. We're coming in to take you out."

It was still snowing off and on. Around 2:00 p.m., we got the call. "Sorry, can't fly today. Will try tomorrow."

So we had to set camp back up—wet and frozen.

The next day came and ended the same way. "Sorry, can't fly today. Will try tomorrow."

So we set camp up again. "Pack up and get ready." The response in camp was "screw you" and "call me when they land."

At around 1000, we heard them coming. It was a little foggy but starting to clear. When the first one landed, we rushed to break camp and get gear netted up.

When the hot food stopped coming, a couple of guys thought they would starve to death—even though we had cases of MREs. The more the weather got bad, the more some panicked more. Morale in camp for some was really low. The crew boss didn't lose it though. Experience paid off for him. I was amazed how some acted when the first hot meal didn't show up. Then rain and snow. We always had hot coffee though. MREs were meant to be heated up, but some weren't used to doing for themselves. Our only temporary problem was we hadn't got lifted out yet—not food; we had plenty. To some it was the end of the world. No TO, phones, or computers.

When the weather hit us, we stayed in camp. But some of us wanted something to do. There was nothing to do in camp but sleeping. It was boring! I went on a hike with five other guys to see what the fire line looked like. On one of our hikes, we ran into a flock of ptarmigans. The crew boss had okayed our hikes with some restrictions: full fire fear, tools, and radio. At first on seeing the flock, we were going to throw rocks at them. A quick discussion and we decided 6 Pulaskis would be better. One, two, three, and all six of us were flying at the birds. Killed three, wounded one—which we easily caught and killed. The proud hunters returned with fresh food. Four weren't nearly enough for twenty some of us. We prepared the birds and cooked them over the fire. It smelled great and tasted good! One guy and one gal said they weren't "going to eat *that!*" But they did try some; I think the smell got to them. Everybody got some.

After dinner, the crew boss got me alone and said, "The birds were good!"

"Yeah, wasn't enough for everyone."

"Can't have you guys killing game out here. We have tons of MREs to eat."

"Actually, a lot of MREs were eaten with the bird meat."

"Ritchey, you're the oldest guy on this crew and some are following your lead. You know that, right?"

"Hadn't really thought about it that way—guess you're right."

"I don't know if I could get them out of camp in shit weather like this, and they work for me. You got a third of the camp to take a hike with you.

"Yeah, but that's different."

Then loudly and most heard him say, *"Different?* How the heck do you figure?"

"Well, going with you would be work—going with me would be fun," I said in an embarrassed tone.

I was embarrassed when he yelled, *"Different?* How the heck… figure?" Because I looked around and saw some of the crew watching us. They had heard "that" plain as day.

Then just as loud, he asked, "Who the heck's idea was it?"

Darn, I couldn't tell if he was ticked or kidding me. "Is it a problem?" I asked.

"Just might be," he said

"Well, if it will get me out of here any faster, it was my idea." Then I smiled.

"Come on," he said. And we walked away farther from camp. "That's what I mean—that's why they like you, good sense of humor, always doing something. Tomorrow most of the crew is going to want to be on your hike. I wouldn't be surprised if you brought back a deer or elk! However, no more killing game and we'll pass on the hike tomorrow, okay?"

"Sure, understand."

"Let's go back," he said. As we walked back, he said, "Everyone in camp thinks I'm chewing your ass out and not thanking you for giving the crew a shot in the arm and boosting morale. We need to let them think I chewed your butt out. Okay?"

"Don't understand."

"They need a friend in the ranks. I'm going to get you bumped up to AD-3 and squad boss."

"Wow! Thanks! Wait, why don't you socialize more with them, make friends?"

"I need the respect, not the friendship."

Oh. I went back to my tent thinking, *What the heck does that mean?* Later on, in my career, I would realize how deep those words of wisdom were, and they came from a guy ten years younger than me but with ten years more experience.

*****

We finally got sent back to Harlowton and given "time-occupying jobs." Boring! Was about forty or more ADs that were there waiting for fires to be sent to. About five of the Glacier crew said it was enough and quit. So we got replacements for those who left—to keep our crew of twenty. Shortly after the Glacier fire, Yellowstone Park caught on fire. It actually started in Idaho, and they put it out up to the park's land. We wanted to go but were held back for a while. Then I found out the Parks Service policy was "Let it burn!" Finally, we got orders to go and were bussed down—all of us!

Couldn't go right to work. Had to learn the rules—all six million rules of the Park Service. Park Service asked who could run chainsaws and I raised my hand with some others. With some review of the running of a chainsaw, we were ready to go. We had a Park Service Ranger put with our crew named Sue. Lord, have mercy! Couldn't start a chainsaw, let alone cut something without her knowing all the details of what you were thinking and her personal okay.

Never realized how big and destructive fire could be till I got into Yellowstone in '88. It was surreal—really! Having a policy of "Let it burn" didn't help either.

They realized that letting it burn was out of hand. The cost that summer was $74 million to the Forest Service Northern Region by September 20, 1988. Just under 5 million gallons of retardant was dropped on the fires. (Facts from Northern Region, Summer of '88)

Area men part of forest fire fighting crews

by Julia DeBuff

Bob Ritchey spent nine days fighting fire in the Bob Marshall Wilderness area. The crew left Harlo on Saturday morning, September 10, at 4:00 a.m. by bus for Choteau where they picked up Johnny Taber and other members of his crew, and the entire group was taken to the fire line by helicopters.

Camp was first set up at Gates Park. Shortly after they got set up it began to rain. However, when they got up Sunday morning there was some 4 inches of snow on the ground.

On Monday, 12th, the camp was moved eight miles further in by choppers to Sun River Pass area, and set up again. Tuesday all the crews were out patrolling and putting out small fires. They walked some 10 miles that day. However, when they went back in on Wednesday, they found many of the small fires they thought they had extinguished had caught up again. Even though the fire appeared to be put out, it still smoldered in the stumps, and in the foot-deep bed of pine needles that had fallen and packed down for many years.

Thursday, the 15th, the whole crew was on the fire line and had a rather bad time of it because the fire crowned, burning in the tops of the trees and spreading fast. The choppers were bringing in retardant and water to help control the blaze, and as Bob watched one coming in, it flew directly over him, dumping its load of water. A lot of water hit him directly, soaking him completely, but the fire was being brought under control.

Friday, the 16th, was spent mostly in patrolling hot spots and putting them out. Lines were dug around the fire completely down to the earth, through a foot or more of packed needles, and a couple feet wide.

Sometime before the firefighters got there, the Wrong Creek Ranger Station was completely destroyed by the fire. Bob took several pictures of the remains of the cabin, as well as of the area where the fire was burning.

The choppers were to have gone to the camp on Saturday, the 17th, but the overcast was too heavy, and there was the probability of heavy snow, so they did not get there. That day the crew walked nine miles to the fireline through rain at first, then snow. After the day spent in patrolling and checking for hot spots, they walked the nine miles back to camp. They got in late, but found a hot meal waiting for them, with lots of hot coffee to warm them up.

Of the 20 men in the party, seven had colds by Saturday. However, none were serious at the time. The choppers came in on Sunday and brought out the entire party, and they returned to Harlo late Sunday evening.

Bob said he flew in so many helicopters that he didn't know where he was going when they left, didn't know where he was when they got there, and didn't know where he had been when he got back.

RANGER STATION BURNED! This is the remains of the "Wrong Creek" Ranger Station which was completely destroyed by one of the recent forest fires. (Photo by Bob Ritchey)

So I ran a chainsaw and on the first day found out why they get paid more. Not only did I have to keep my fire gear on, but was now carrying another pack with fuel, oil, files, extra saw parts, and a chainsaw.

"Sue" and I only had one bad run-in. She stopped us on a steep mountainside one day and wanted me to cut enough wood for the crew to put in twenty-one water bars—four stakes, two inches long—to hold a log across a trail to prevent erosion. Looked like this:

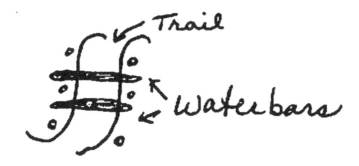

trail, water bars

How close together depended on the steepness of the terrain. Sue and the crew went on to the bottom, and I started cutting the water bars. I had about half done of the twenty-one when one of the crew came back up. He told me Sue changed her mind about the bars. I was to catch up with them. He returned to the crew and I put everything away and packed up.

I went down three hundred feet of a steep side, where the water bars were to go, with all my gear. When I got to the bottom, I saw the crew coming back toward me.

Sue came over to me and said, "I guess we are going to put the water bars in. Need you to go back up and finish cutting them!" The crew would be digging the ruts for the logs to sit in on the trail

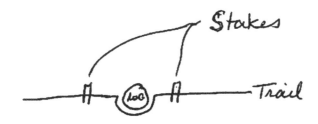

stakes, trail

and work their way back up to me. I had to give her a piece of my mind and said, "Lady, I'm going to carry all this crap back up and finish the bars. But if you call me back down, I won't go back up. Understand?"

*****

We stood there a few seconds face to face. I don't know what I saw in her eyes—didn't like it though. Never saw *that* in a woman's eyes before! She finally broke her silence by saying, "Get the f—— up that mountain!" Caught me off guard. I started to smile then turned and went up that "f——" mountain.

I think I said her statement to myself the whole way back up—and laughed the whole way up. It made the trip easier, except when I was laughing so much, I would slide down some.

After our run-in, I made it a point to leave when I'd see her coming around. If we were on a break sitting down together, when she'd come over, I'd get up and walk away. For two days, I don't think I said a word to her even when she talked to me. On the third day, we were all sitting, taking a break, and laughing when I saw her coming. I stood and started to walk off when she said, "Bob, you might want to hear this." It was said nicely, so I returned.

Late that night, I was sitting by myself making a cup of coffee over a fire. She came up behind me and said, "Bob." I spilled some of the coffee in the fire and on me. All I could say was "Damn, damn."

She was trying to hold in a laugh—and finally she said, "I'm sorry," laugh, laugh. I kind of chuckled. Must've looked like an idiot. I was still holding my pants away from my body.

I said, "I'll dry."

"No," she said, "for the other day and the water bars." Heck, that's okay. Then she chuckled some more and looked at my lap.

I was still holding my pants away. When I asked if she was sorry for this too, she lost it. I must have tried to say "yes" four or five times before it came out as a laughing "yes." She was laughing so much, it brought tears to her eyes. I asked her if she wanted some coffee. "No." She stayed a while, while I made another cup of coffee and we just BSed.

We were in Yellowstone until November 6, and then we went back to Harlowton so we could vote on November 7. Then we returned to Yellowstone for another two weeks. We went from fire to fire throughout Yellowstone. It was a long fire season! Spent almost six months in Yellowstone.

*****

The next year, I was offered a contract with a GS-3 rating, which I jumped at. Permanent part-time, noncompetitive rehire. Six months guaranteed employment per year and six months off. Ideal! A GS-3 paid a lot less than an AD-4, but on a fire, I made a lot more than ADs, plus I got comp and sick time. Later I became road foreman for our mountain rangers and got a GS-4 rating. When fires started, I was a firefighter. I qualified for engineer boss, crew boss, squad boss, B Sawyers, and got into a new program called IMS (incident medical specialist), medical division. I had become a county EMT on my six months off. And I took the course with the Sioux Indians. With getting into IMS, the crew started calling me "Doc." Really liked that nickname!

A lot of the guys in Harlowton and Stanford trained for a "Smoke Chaser" crew. We trained at the Missoula Smoke Jump Center, and they weeded guys out like crazy. Didn't know if this "old man" could survive this. Smoke Jumpers were the trainers for the Smoke Chasers. The Jumpers were the elite and toughest of the Forest Service. At the time, there were thirty thousand firefighters and four hundred Smoke Jumpers in the US. The first week was brutal with long days. A lot of people who tried out either quit or were weeded out. I hung in there...some days hoping for a massive coronary. When the Smoke Jumpers were done with us, we were a tough, close-knit group of guys. We were initial attack crews and I was a medic for them. When the fire started, we went in and hit it hard till ground-pounders got there. We flew a lot, mostly by choppers. They'd set us down and we'd hit the fire. We weren't Smoke Jumpers. We were a cross between Smoke Jumpers and the Hot Shots. The

Smoke Chasers got a newly designed red line pack to replace the yellow line pack that the ground-pounders wore. Our helmets were red, not yellow, same as our personal gear pack. Now we really felt special. On many fires, we claimed as getting there first, some Jumpers would already be there. I liked being with the Jumpers a lot. I liked being with J. Don't know how, but they always had the best food with them. I made some good friends with some Jumpers. I lost one at Stone Mountain fire in Colorado. There were too many deaths there. Any death was too many anywhere. Being "Doc," I would usually be on the first flight in. In case of a crash, I'd be there already, unless it was one, I was in. Usually, three or four flights would get the whole crew in to the fire.

During one fire, the weather got "iffy." Four of us went on the first flight in. We flew to the top of a mountain, our starting point. It was pretty bumpy going up. When we started to land, the wind caught us. It felt like the chopper was flying on its side for a few seconds. The pilot told us to get ready to throw the equipment out. He lowered to about twenty feet and out it went. He moved away from the equipment and said he couldn't set it down. We would have to jump, so we did—all of five to six feet. Then he took off. We almost said it together, "We're Jumpers." We jumped from a chopper! While we were getting things ready for the next group of guys to arrive, we heard our pilot talking to the airport. He didn't think he could make another flight up there—"dropped equipment and four crew, okay, but about kissed the mountain doing it!" Then it hit us. We came really close to crashing. Our excitement about jumping from a chopper quickly faded. It was the first and only close call I ever had in a chopper and we flew a lot.

We had all the tools for the crew and our line packs and nothing else. The fire was three miles away and about twelve to fifteen miles to where we took off from, and mountains and timber in between. We got a hold of base and asked what they wanted us to do. "Hold tight, we'll get back to you." About an hour later, we got our call. Lucky I wasn't on the radio. We were told to "Return to base."

"Return to base? How?"

"You're going to have to walk out."

"Do you know how far that is?"

The dispatcher (a woman) said, "Yes…pilot said 8.6 miles."

"Yeah, as the crow flies! It's probably twice that far walking. There's at least two mountains between you and us."

You're going to have to walk it, I'm sorry. Everything's grounded. There are no roads near you. I'm sorry. Base also wants you to do a radio check every hour and give your location."

"Ten-four!"

"Base out."

The good news was it was 0930 and half the trip would be down mountainsides. The bad news was the other half of the trip would be up mountainsides. Would be lucky in this timber to do a mile-per-hour. We did have a compass, direction reading to travel, and head lamps—the basics. We had some flares and decided to take four Pulaskis with us. So off we went. At around 1400, we built a small fire and heated some MRSs to eat and made some coffee. Did the same at around 2000. We were still walking at 0230. We should have arrived by now. We were going to call base, then we decided not to yet. One guy went up a tree. "Lights to right, maybe half a mile, maybe a mile. Looks like base!" Thank God! At 0300, we weren't quite there but could see base, at 0305 base called us. "SC location?" Best response I ever heard someone say… "Coming in your back door. ETA, two minutes." "Check in at communication tent when you get here. Glad you're back." Us too!

We were still talking on the radio as we entered the communication tent. We were all GSs, so after eight hours, we got time and a half, plus flight and hazard pay for the whole time, and never saw the fire that day! I wouldn't do that trip again for twice the money. All of us went to the mess tent after the comm tent. Got coffee and mixed cocoa packs with it. I slept on the tables till the crews started to come in for breakfast.

We decided to eat breakfast. We were pointed out to the IC (incident commander). He came over and asked how we were doing and apologized for not being able to get us out. "Anything you need or want, just ask." We all said "sleep!" "You got it! Your crew stayed at the airport till 1200 yesterday, then back to camp. Will probably do the same today. Weather. You guys stay in and get some rest."

He started laughing. "That was dumb to say," then he left. We hadn't moved to the line to get breakfast yet and were still drinking coffee and cocoa again. Then some food staff came over with four trays of food. Steak (real steak), two eggs (also real), and pancakes. "IC told us to make this for you guys." Everyone else got "mystery" meat. I slept all day till 1600, showered, and went to mess tent—coffee with cocoa packs.

DEARBORN FIRE

The Dearborn fire was around the Helena area and while there, an "event" happened I never told anyone about. I was doing the "line medic" thing—walking the fire lines between crews checking for injuries. It was around 0030 when I came on a crew coming out of a fire area. They were coughing, stumbling out, could tell something had happened to them. I found the crew boss and tried talking to him. The crew had inhaled a lot of smoke. All were having trouble getting the smoke out and the good air in. Some laid down coughing, some standing, some sitting, and some walking around. They couldn't really talk because of the coughing. I was trying to get the story of what happened from the crew boss when three more came out, hacking away and joining us about a hundred feet from where they came out. I counted heads—fifteen guys, five short of a full crew. I asked the crew boss how many in his crew. He gave me ten fingers, twice.

"Not twenty-one?"

He shook his head *no*.

"You had fifteen guys?" Shook his head no again and gave me ten fingers twice again.

"Where's the rest?" He tried saying "coming" but couldn't, pointing instead to where they had come out of.

I went to the last three who had come out. "Where's the others?" Two of the three-pointed back to the trail. The third was throwing up.

I dropped my line pack—kept my fire shelter belt on. I went to the trail and started back in looking for the missing five.

Ten feet in, I decided I needed a wet bandanna on my face. I went back to my pack and poured water on my bandanna and put it on my nose and mouth area. I went back in on the trail. I was hot and on fire but could make my way through it okay. Not sure how far back in I went—hundred feet, maybe two hundred? Suddenly, I realized how quiet it was in here. The heat was not only bearable but actually felt kind of nice. It was between 12:30 and 1:00 a.m., but the trail was bright from the flames. I thought, *God, this is like a maze in here.* I could only see fifteen to twenty feet ahead, then a turn. At the last turn, I walked into an area that just amazed me. To me it seemed to be a circle area—lined the whole way around by large trees. They seemed so close together that nothing could get through them. It was like day in there—everything had a beautiful orange, yellow, and red tint to it. I looked up and it was almost like the area had a roof on it, which naturally was on fire. No sound, felt nice in here—*so peaceful, it's wonderful,* I thought. Beautiful. Suddenly, my knees hit the ground and I was on all fours.

I shook my head a couple of times and came back to reality. The roar of the fire was deafening; warmth was now uncomfortably hot. The area was smoky with swirls. Still on all fours, I realized the oxygen in here was really low. Really low! I saw two firefighters with their heads on their legs, two lying flat out about ten feet apart, and one on all fours and trying to move toward me. I went over to the first lying down—he had a pulse, but couldn't bring him around. I checked the others—all alive. The second one lying down came around when I shook him. I got him to start crawling out. The other one on all fours seemed to pep up upon seeing me and now the other one was moving, so he was following him out the trail.

I crawled over and tried to lift one who was in a sitting position. Deadweight! Couldn't lift him. I pushed him and the other into laying positions. I recognized him but didn't know his name. I grabbed his fire shelter but the swirls whipped it around, so I just tucked it under and over his head and arms. I was wasting time I didn't have. I was only going to save the moving two. The two who were crawling hadn't gone very far and were hardly moving. I caught up with them

in seconds. We crawled. I remember turning my head and seeing the three I had left. This is bullshit—I jumped to my feet and grabbed the guy ahead of me and jerked him to his feet. I pushed him ahead of the others. I did the same with the other. I don't know how, but I just kept pushing them—if and when they fell. I yelled and jerked them back up and pushed them. I finally got them out and laid them down.

A couple of their crew walked over to us. We were doing better, but in no condition to help get the other three. I saw a bunch of headlamps coming around the south end of the fire toward us. They weren't far from us. I went over to them and said, "I need six of you to come with me." "F—— you" and "Go screw yourself" were some of the responses.

The crew boss came up to me and said, "what do you want?" I realized I still had my bandanna over my face, so I pulled it down. "I need six of your best and strongest guys. I got three guys down just inside the fire line. Need to get them out." He called off some names and told them to go with me and help. They had kept on walking while I was trying to get them to help. So we were almost to the trail when he called out the names to go with me. I told them to wet something and cover their faces—no tools or packs, fire shelters only.

As I turned to take the six in, the crew boss grabbed my arm. "How far in?"

"A hundred feet or so."

"Don't make me come get you. In and out—in and out."

In we went and very quickly were picking up the three. Was probably only fifty feet into them, two firefighters picking up one each and carrying them out. I doubt if it took five minutes and all three were out. Bad shape, but alive and not burned. I knew now I had lost it going in, low oxygen, and had probably been standing in there thinking I was moving. It threw a fear in me that the fire "touched" me like that.

I called base and gave our location and quickly explained what I had. They sent three Suburbans to us and one ambulance. The crew got in two of the three Suburbans. The ambulance crew and I loaded the last three and they took them to Helena Hospital. I think the driver of the third Suburban helped load them up also. The crew that got smoked was taken to the medical tent to be checked out. The crew that helped get the last three out disappeared into camp, I guess. At the end, it was just me and the driver of the third Suburban.

"Didn't get a chance to thank the crew that helped," I said.

As I was watching the ambulance lights disappear, the third Suburban driver said, "I'm going back to camp. Need a ride?"

"Yeah, let me find my pack."

Walked up the hill, grabbed my pack, and went to the suburban. He turned the suburban around when I was coming back. I opened the passenger door. The light was bright. Got in holding my pack and shut the door. The driver turned the inside light on and said, "where'd you get that fancy pack?"

"They were made for our crew."

"What crew is that?"

"Smoke Chasers."

"Never heard of them."

I looked at my watch: 0122? I asked what time the driver had. He said, "0125."

"Drop me off at the med tent."

"You got it!"

The smoked crew was in and around the med tent. As I made my way into the tent to do my report on this, I saw a couple of the guys standing outside smoking a cigarette. Guess they'll make it. Ho-ho.

I got the crew's info and names of the three whom I sent to the hospital and wrote a quick report about it. I included "unknown crew helped." I signed it and turned it in and went to my tent twenty feet from the med tent. I lay in my sleeping bag and was thinking I must have read my watch wrong, the rescue and transporting of the men to the hospital could not have possibly happened in less than an hour.

I thought about when I went in to find those guys. I saw everything as before without sound. To me it felt like I was on that trail

twenty minutes or so before I found them. Got to get more sleep! The oxygen must have gotten sucked out around them and must have been why they went down. I wonder if they saw what I saw and felt like I felt in there.

$$*****$$

About three years later, I was in downtown Harlowton and saw the guy I had recognized in there. Now I knew who he was. "Hey, Brian."

He turned. "Yeah?"

"You were in the Dearborn fire."

"Yeah?"

"I sent you to the hospital."

"Oh yeah, don't remember much about that fire. Thanks!" We stood there staring at each other. I could see "it" in his eyes and he probably saw "it" in my eyes.

"Well, I got to go," I said.

"Me too."

"See you sometime." I started to tum and leave.

"Yeah, hey thanks again."

For a while, I would dream about that wonderful walk-in. When I got to the part when my knees were going to hit the ground, I'd wake with a jolt. Just like a shock. I hated that dream after a while and finally got it stored in my memories.

"The Last Hundred Feet" (The "Chain")

A third of a football field! To some people and animals, this distance is no great task. To a racer at Indy 500, it's a fraction of a second—driving at sixty miles per hour on the highway, just over a second (60 mph = 88 feet per second) to a running deer, under two seconds, to a running bear, just over 2 seconds, to a snail, maybe a lifetime. To a firefighter, it can be life or death. Many firefighters have died trying for that last one hundred feet to get to safety. Some missed it by just feet! How could you not make the last hundred feet if your life depended on it?

I found the USFS in my late thirties and fell into my "niche" in life—fighting forest fires. One of the first things I was asked to do was walk a hundred feet and count my steps. Thirty-seven steps was my count. Was then told that these thirty-seven steps of mine equaled one Forest Service "chain."

A chain was an important piece of information. A firefighter could walk around a small fire, count his steps (chains), and relay this information to his base, along with type of fuel, weather conditions, and terrain.

The number of chains around the fire would give the approximate size of the fire. The Forest Service could get a fairly good idea of the size of the fire, number of firefighters needed, and equipment

needed to fight the fire, just by the numbers of chains of the fire (fifty-three chains equal a mile).

All throughout my career and even now, a hundred feet is only thirty-seven steps to me; to you maybe a few more or a few less. So why have so many failed in their attempt to reach that last hundred feet? It's a fire!

*****

In August 1949, six months after I was born, the Mann Gulch fire started north of Helena, Montana. Sixteen Smoke Jumpers (the elite of USFS) jumped into Mann Gulch to fight the fire. The fire blew up and they had to run for it. They came to their last couple hundred feet to safety. The terrain was not in their favor—but only a hundred feet or so to go. The crew boss decided to try something new: start a grassy area on fire ahead of the main fire and get into its ashes before the main fire hit them. He stopped and lit it. It was working. As his crew caught up to him, he ordered them into the small burnt area. He wanted them to lie down and let the fire burn around them. It would be hot, but the last hundred feet wasn't doable in his mind. Only two of his fifteen crew went in with him. The other thirteen refused and pushed hard for that last hundred feet to safety. The main fire slammed the area fast and had been *hot!* Thirteen died in their tracks in the last hundred feet. The crew boss and the other two lived. The crew boss was credited with the first' safety burn' or 'back-burn' (Young Men and Fire by Norman Maclean).

Decades later, in the '90s and after I joined the UFSF, another fire blew up in Colorado. The fire was called Stone Mountain Fire. It was like Mann Gulch fire in many ways. Crews died there, trying for the last hundred feet! Some bodies were recovered several *feet* from safety! Just a couple more steps to life and they didn't make it. Unbelievable! Why? It's a *fire!* It's fast, hot, and very deadly. When it slams you, you are dead in your tracks! *Dead! In your tracks!* Whether it's a hundred feet or ten feet, you are dead. An inhalation of breath at the wrong time will waste your lungs immediately. I was at the

Yellowstone Park fires in 1988 for six months. While there, we would come across animals—deer, elk, bear—that were many times faster and more alert to danger than man…burnt to a crisp! They couldn't outrun the fire. So why does man think he can? Thank God someone invented the famous "shake and bake" fire shelters. They do give you a chance if you can find the right terrain, heavy timber *not* being one. Temps in the shelters hit 150 degrees, but then outside, it can sail over 800 degrees. At 800 degrees and above, everything burns and the "shake and bakes" do hold up!

I was burned over twice in "shake and bakes." The first time was exciting! We made it to a small clearing out of the timber. We had enough time to clear the area of fuel (burnable) and deploy our shelters. The fire burnt over us and passed us. Shortly after, we were given the "all clear" and came out in great shape. It was great, they were great, they work!

The second time was a whole new ball game! I was about to learn a lot about fire and "shake and bakes." We were in heavy timber, steep mountains of the Rockies. We were at a point that our main concern was not just staying ahead of the fire but trying to outrun it. The wind had changed and closed our escape route. We finally came to a narrow mountain dirt road. As we came down the one bank, with the fire on our heels, our crew boss gave the order to deploy our shelters on the road. We were in a gulley filled with smoke, with a steep bank on one side, the narrow dirt road, and then another steep bank up. We barely got in our shelters before it hit us. Because the road was so narrow, we couldn't put two shelters side by side. We had twenty shelters in a line. This was going to be a *hot* one and it was!

The temperature went up in the shelters, it became almost unbreathable. The winds of the fire grab the shelter and it's all you can do to hold it down, then it snaps the shelters down against you. Your fingers turn white; you're holding on so tight. The sound is like having a train go right over you. This wasn't to be a short time in the shelters. As I laid there hanging on to my shelter, listening to the almost unbearable sound of the fire, I thought I could hear bombs

exploding around me. When I emerged, I would find out what the noise was.

Finally, the wind and noise passed. I don't know how long it lasted, seemed like hours. I was completely exhausted from trying to keep my shelter down. It was a long time coming until we got the "all clear" to come out. Actually, I think it was cooler in the shelter than out. The area had certainly changed since I had gotten in my shelter. I looked around. The trees had burnt, some still smoldering, and some looked like they were blown apart. Here and there in the ground, it looked like a bomb had dropped and exploded.

There were different size holes. I found out later that at around three hundred degrees, trees explode and at five hundred degrees, rocks explode We were lucky; only 1 injury. A tree had burned off the one bank and rolled across one shelter, poking holes in it. He had some burns on his leg. While we were in the shelters, lunch had come and long passed. We spent most of that day on the road in shelters. After that, I never wanted to be in one again. It wasn't exciting this time!

THAT DAY

I think many people, at least here in America, cruise through their lives with the normal ups and downs, never having to make the decision to live or die.

I remember reading that a lot of people who are kidnapped, one way or another, will get out of the vehicle and walk into the woods, doing everything the man (person) behind them with the gun says to do. They never try to at least do something to save their life. They go willingly to their death, believing it won't—can't—happen to them.

I remember hearing an astronaut answer questions about his upcoming spacewalk. It was early in our space program. The reporter asked him what he would do if his space suit got a hole in it and he had only ten seconds to fix it or die. The astronaut didn't answer right away, but you could tell his mind was going a million miles per hour, pondering the problem posed. He finally answered the reporter, "I'd think it through for nine seconds and act the last second." That's really deep. Think more before you react.

I do know that surviving your last chain is very painful, both mentally and physically. I am one of a handful who made their trip of the last chain and survived. Twenty years later, I still remember my last hundred feet like it was yesterday. Once in a while, a flashback pops in my mind and a segment of that day plays over and over. It is still hard for me to believe that I survived!

I loved fighting fires. It was a challenge trying to outthink a fire. I worked up the GS ladder some in rank. Any training they had available, I took, and they have a lot. During a fire, I was qualified for most positions. I had been a county EMT prior to joining the USFS. And within a year, they decided to create their own medical

unit. It was called IMS (incident medical specialist). There were only two hundred spots in the US in the first year, and I got one. It didn't take the other government agencies long to step in and change a few things. The "incident" was changed to "interagency," and we found ourselves getting more training, new patches.

And now we were on loan to other agencies for any situation, not just fires. Most of us became medics.

Later, they created the "Smoke Chasers." USFS had regular firefighters, Hot Shots, and the elite Smoke Jumpers. The Smoke Chasers were to be a cross between the Hot Shots and the Smoke Jumpers.

About 250 firefighters applied for forty positions. I tried out for it, two weeks of long days of brutal training in Missouri under Smoke Jumpers supervision. They weeded us out by half the first day! It was tough, tough training. At the end of two weeks, I found myself on one of the two twenty-man crews. The Hot Shots walked in to the fires, the Smoke Jumpers jumped into the fires, the Smoke Chasers flew into fires by choppers. The Smoke Chasers were sent to helicopter training, not to learn how to fly, but all training was about them, including landing them…just in case? I liked that! So now I was in my forties, was a Smoke Chaser, and a medic.

When I wasn't fighting fires, I was the road foreman for our district: Crazy Mountains, Castle Mountains, Big Snowy Mountains, Little Snowy Mountains, and the Belts. I had a crew of five that worked for me. I loved it—in the mountains every day and got paid for it. I learned the mountains well. All the different departments of the USFS wore their fire clothes and carried their fire gear with them. In case of fire, everyone was ready to go. I had four packs: fire pack, medical pack, sawyer pack and saw, and my miscellaneous pack.

Every once in a while, I'd get a call to go check for a "smoke" that someone thought they saw, so we'd stop the roadwork and go and try to find it.

*****

It was just one of those beautiful days in the Rocky Mountains of Montana, early in the fire season. I love the smell of the Rocky Mountain pines; it is indescribably fresh and healthy.

My crew of five and I had arrived around 0800 at our point of work and were doing some minor pothole fills on a small section of Forest Service land, when I got a call from our base.

Base: Ritchey. Harlowton.
Me: Harlowton. Ritchey. Go. Over.
Base: Ten-twenty? Over (location you are at).
Me: Past Cooks flats, between 10+11 markers. Over.
Harlo Base: Received smoke report. Your area. Can you check
    Southeast, two to five miles your location for smoke? Over.
Me: Ten-four. Loading now. Over.
Harlo Base: Harlowton out.

The crew was elated to stop the shovel work and go look for a smoke. We loaded out shovels in the bed of one truck. My truck was a Wildland pumper unit, carrying two hundred gallons of water, plus hoses, tools, and emergency gear. The other truck was a standard cab, full size Chevy. My crew, since we worked in the mountains every day, always wore their fire clothes. And we always had our line great with us to fight fires. The excitement was high that we might find a fire. The crews were trained to fight fires but did other work until a fire showed up. It was a good feeling working with others who wanted to fight fires and were trained to do it.

We were high up and in tall timber, hard to see in the distance. At any clearings, we stopped and binoc'd the area for smoke. Drove and stopped, drove and stopped. After twenty to thirty minutes, one of the crew spotted it and we worked our way to it. It was about a hundred yards from a side road we took. The side road, opened into a small open area with few trees. We stopped the trucks on the road, got out, and looked across the open area, about a hundred yards. The fire was on the side of one of the steep mountains and was two hundred to three hundred feet up the side.

Me: Harlowton. Ritchey.

Harlo Base: Ritchey. Harlowton. Go.

Me: Located smoke. Area approximate. E-3 Map 119. Over.

Harlo Base: Size of fire? Over.

Me: Ten to twenty acres. Over. (I always hated giving size of a fire. Was always terrible at guessing it.)

Harlo Base: Can you get pumper to it? Over.

Me: Negative. Heavy timber. Extremely steep. Over.

Harlo Base: Condition of fire? Over.

Me: Flames burning. Not doing much. Wind is calm. Smoke straight up. Over.

Harlo Base: What do you need? Over.

Me: One or two crews, I extra…

Harlo Base: Ritchey. Break. Over. ("Break" is a polite way of saying "be quiet" or "shut up.")

About a minute later, Harlowton Base called back.

Harlo Base: Ritchey. Harlowton.

Me: Go Harlowton. Ritchey. Over.

Harlo Base: Great Falls has fixed-wing leaving now to spot from air. What do you need? Over.

Me: One or two crews. One extra pumper. Twenty piss pumps (bags that carried five gallons of water with a hand pump sprayer). Over.

Harlo Base: Anything else? Over.

Me: Yes, make that two to three crews. Two pumpers. ASAP. Over. (Prime burn time was 1000 to 1600. It was now at 0915. Fires seem to really burn between 10:00 a.m. and 4:00 p.m.)

Harlo Base: Ten-four. Twenty *loading now.* ETA 60, 20 + pumper in Crazies. ETA 120, 20 + pumper in Castles. ETA 0, 60 to 90. Over.

Me: Better get sixty on standby. Over.

Harlo Base: Fire condition changing? Over.

Me: No, still calm. Gut feeling. Over.

Harlo Base: Ten-four. 60+ 2 on way. Base wants road flagged from known landmark. Find safety zone and flag it. Call with locations of each.

Me: Ten-four. Harlowton. Over.

I sent Lori and Jarret to mile marker 10 to start flagging route to fire. Jim and Al went to locate and flag safety zone. Lori and Jarret took the pickup and left. Joe drove Jim and Al in the pumper to find a safety zone and flag. Joe was to drop them off and return to me. Before Joe left, I grabbed my misc. pack out of the pumper. I always had four packs—line gear, sawyer pack with saw, medical pack, and my misc. pack with all things needed at fires.

I relayed this info to Harlowton Base.

Harlo Base: Base wants you to take wind speed, humidity, and temp and call info when you get it. Over.

Me: Anything else? Over.

Harlo Base: Think you can walk the line and flag it? (Walk the line meant walk around the fire.) Give us "chain" number? (A 'chain' equaled the number of steps one takes in one hundred feet. In my case, it was thirty-seven steps per hundred feet.) Over.

Me: (Wasn't really thrilled about doing the walk—rather climb.) Ten-four. When pumper returns, I'll walk the line. Over.

Harlo Base: Reynolds crew, ETA 60. Harlowton out.

Me: Ritchey out.

I took all the readings. Decided to walk over to the mountain to see what I was getting into. I left my misc. pack on the road where I wanted Joe to stop the pumper. Got about fifty yards closer to it when Joe returned in the pumper. Had a bunch of stuff to go over with Joe before I took off.

I recognized the area, had hunted elk in a park about a mile west of here. (Park is a grassy area with few, if any, trees.) The park was in a saddle and was about a hundred acres or so in size. (Saddle is the down slope of one mountain and the up slope of another.)

As I walked back to the pumper, I stopped and took another look at the fire. Still calm but burning. At least it wasn't crowning (crowning is the fire jumping from tree top to tree top). I could see the potential for this fire to really blow up. It was growing, but very slowly. The prime burn time wasn't here yet.

Joe told me the safety zone was 2.4 miles back. Poor grass area, few trees. We marked it on our map.

"You want to flag the fire, Joe?"

"Sure."

"Know how to work all this gear?"

"No."

I laughed. "I better do it."

Gave Joe a pair of binocs and instructions to stay with the pumper. I'd be talking to him on work channel #3. We had fourteen channels—all monitored by Great Falls, our state regional office.

"You watch me through these binocs. Don't let me walk toward the fire. Okay?"

"Ten-four."

"You call me right away if anything changes, flare ups, the smoke blowing differently, any change. Want to know if the picture we are looking at now changes in anyway. I'm putting my life in your hands—you are my eyes from now on."

"Got it!"

"Okay, let's mark the map." I spread it out on the ground. "Here's where I'm going up the mountain. Point A." I marked it A. "I'll be going straight up to those rock outcroppings. Point B. You see them?"

"Yes."

"That's point C. It should take me across the top of the fire safely from point B." (Straight down from point C was point D where I would come out and off the mountain.)

We marked all the points on the map and returned to the pumper.

We put rocks on the corners of the map and we spread it out again. I grabbed a notepad.

"Joe, if I tell you to move point B a hundred feet up and a hundred feet west, don't move the original point B on the map. Do it this way." I drew on the pad:

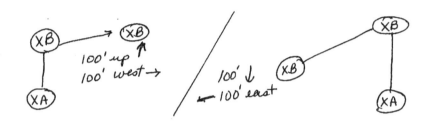

"When I give you my location, mark it on the map with an R and track me between the points. Understand?"

"Yeah, it's simple!"

Walking to point A, I did a radio check with Joe on Channel 3.

Me: Joe. Ritchey.

Joe: Ritchey. Joe. Go.

Me: Reading me okay?

Joe: Ten-four.

Me: Just came to a long ditch about thirty feet wide and twenty feet deep right before point A. Mark that on the map.

Joe: How do I do that?

Me: Draw a line under point A about two inches long. Put arrowheads at each end and then write Ditch 30' W 20'D—full of high dry grass, HDG. Understand?

Joe: Ten-four. It's done.

Me: I'll be using blue and white flagging to line the fire. Write that on the map somewhere.

Joe: Ten-four.

Me: I took reading for Harlowton. They are on a notepad in pumper. Call Harlowton and give info to them on Channel 7. Leave pumper radio on, scan, and then come back to channel 3. Okay?

Joe: Ten-four.

Me: I'll take another reading between B and C.
Joe: Ten-four.

Humidity was still up at the base of the mountain. I knew that would change shortly. I listened to Joe giving info to Harlowton and he did a good job of doing it. Ah crap! Forgot to start counting my steps for the first chain…close enough. Chain 1. Ha!

As I was flagging from point A to B, the flagging hung straight down. No wind, good. You don't want it blowing toward you. That means you're in front of the fire. Not good!

Walking the line, counting the chains, would give base the app size and dimension of the fire. The readings at the base and top of the fire would give base "conditions" of the fire—all needed to fight a fire effectively with the correct number of people and equipment.

Joe: Doc, can't see you! ("Doc" being my nickname.)
Me: That's okay. I can't see you either. Ha! I'm four chains up on A+B line, heavy timber and smoke. Steep! Mark me on the map. (I was noticing a little flag movement on my last flag. Was west toward me.)
Me: Joe, how's point A+B. Can you still see?
Joe: Ten-four. But is kind of hazy.
Me: Point B is hazy.
Joe: Ten-four. Points A+ B are hazy.
Me: A+ B?
Joe: Ten-four.
Me: Is the smoke heading west?
Joe: Kind of.
Me: That's a yes or no question, Joe!
Joe: Ten-four. West slowly.
Me: Yes or no, Joe. Is point A *smoky?*
Joe: Ten-four. Very smoky now.
Me: Joe, walk down to where we looked and marked C and D. See what those points look like and come right back and tell me what they look like.

Joe: Ten-four.

I thought to myself, *Crap, the ditch is on fire.* Joe wouldn't see the fire, just the smoke from the road.

Joe didn't have a radio. He was using the pumper radio. While he was checking C and D out, I decided I better widen out a little. Moved west a chain from the A to B line. He still hadn't called me back as I started climbing up again. It was tough going. Wasn't a lot of ground fuel (deadfall), but some. There was a lot of "Duff" (pine needles, etc. that build up inches deep and, once on fire, can burn for days or weeks underground before coming up as fire). I dug where I was at. There was about ten inches deep of this crap. Not good.

Joe: Doc?
Me: How's C and D look?
Joe: C is clear as before—no smoke. D has a lot of smoke now, can't actually see our mark. All the smoke is heading west.
Me: Toward A?
Joe: Ten-four.
Me: Joe, I moved a hundred feet west and am heading up again. Over halfway up now. Mark it!
Joe: Ten-four.
Me: Look around. Can you see me or point B?

Before Joe answered, Harlowton called me.

Harlo: Ritchey. Harlowton.
Me: Go ahead, Harlowton.
Harlo: Reynolds crew leaving. ETA 60. Flag color to fire? Over.
Me: Call Lori on four. Over.
Harlo: Ten-four. Any movement of fire?
Me: Ten-four. Fire moving west with possible blow up in east lower corner. Is a ditch before Mountain "HDG" in it. Think it ignited. Lots, if some. Over.
Harlo: Stand by, Ritchey

About two minutes later…

Harlo: Ritchey. Harlowton.
Me: Harlowton. Ritchey. Go. Over.
Harlo: You are to return to pumper and safety zone. Crews on their way. Over.
Me: I can't go back down. Point of entry is covered by smoke. Know there are flames there. Have to go west. Over.
Harlo: What are you thinking? Over.
Me: West! Straight across! Then either up and over at the saddle or down if I see a place to get through. Over.

Just then, I heard a plane go over.

Me: Harlo. Just heard a plane above me.
Harlo: Ten-four. Ritchey. Stand by.

Stand by? I called Joe on channel 3 and told him to get in the pumper and go to the safety zone and tie in with the Reynolds crew.

Joe: Ten-four. How you going to get there?
Me: I'll have to walk it out. How's the fire looking now?
Joe: All smoke. Heavy.
Me: Safety zone, Joe!
Joe: Ten-four.
Harlo: Ritchey. Harlowton.
Me: Harlowton. Ritchey.
Harlo: Pilot says lots of smoke. Crowning north side of mountain. Flames east side of smoke. Possible finger fires at base of mountain. Over.
Me: Ten-four. The ditch I crossed has ignited. I'm heading for a park app one mile west of me in a saddle. I'll cross over there to the south side of mountain. Two- to three-mile walk to road. I'll walk out. Over.
Harlo: You are to get to safety zone. Over.

Me: I can't make the safety zone! Fire is east of me and below me, even with me and ahead of me now. Over.

Harlo: Stand by, Ritchey.

Crap! I hate hearing standby! I wasted a lot of time talking on the radio. I should've been walking and talking—like I could do that on this steep SOB mountain. Being pissed off gave me a new surge of energy and off I took.

I really screwed up. My line gear was still in the pumper! Didn't even have gloves. The shelter would do me no good in this terrain and timber. After about five minutes of heading west, I stopped and took off my misc. pack. I dumped it out. A pair of leather gloves! Great! The rest was of no use to me, so I left it. Didn't need to be carrying thirty-plus pounds of extra weight. Put the gloves on and took off again.

I kept checking behind me and below me for flames. Smoke was breathable, but everything was starting to take a toll on me. The smoke, temp, altitude, and the steepness of the mountain, all starting to hit me. I stopped to tuck my pant legs in my boots. *I'm too old to be doing this bullshit,* I told myself. I undid my laces and tucked my pant legs in and relaced them. I looked behind me and could see it crowning three hundred to four hundred yards behind me. I could tell by the smoke. Seems like that's far, but with a fire, nothing's far. I have seen a fire do a quarter mile in seconds. It still had smoke but wasn't as heavy now. It could mean I was making headway or the flames were growing and sucking it out.

I looked down the mountain and could see flames. Crap, it was catching me from behind and now coming up to me from below. Well, going down was out of the question.

I think this was when I knew I was screwed. I was running out of time. I might make the park but wouldn't make going over to the south side of the mountain. The park was around a hundred acres as I remembered. Hopefully, the elk and deer had been there and the grass would be short. My mind was trying to sort info. I had to come up with something. Finally, just like a casino line game, the

right pieces came together. I'd burn the park and create a big safety zone. I'd light the park grass. It would burn west and leave an area of about a hundred acres with nothing to burn. I'd light it and go back in the timber until the grass fire was far enough in the park. Then I'd go into the burned-up area. The timber fire couldn't touch me then.

I reached for my pack to get a couple of flares. Crap! Didn't remember seeing any flares in it anyway—my lighter had it and one and a half cigarettes. I can do it, but it was going to be tough with a lighter to get it burning good.

Harlo: Ritchey. Harlowton.
Me: Ritchey. Go ahead. Over.
Harlo: Great Falls is calling in. Hello. One crew for fire. Can you
    make it to safety zone yet?
Me: Flames behind and below me. Smoke closing. Over.
Harlo: Location? Over.
Me: Don't know. Half a mile from park?

Just then, I heard the plane go over.

Me: Harlo, just heard the plane again.
Harlo: Ritchey. Standby.

Stand by, my ass! I was heading west for that park, and now I had a plan. This was going to be a little tricky, starting a fire in front of me with one behind me and one below me. With no time to make it over the mountain—damn, was this my best chance? All I needed was a few things in my favor—this is doable! I need enough time to get to the park. Need the grass in the park to be under a foot high so it would burn hot and fast. I needed my lighter to work. I didn't want to try and get something that's *on* fire from the fire. I didn't have time to spare; would be dangerous too. Needed to find that park. Hoped I wouldn't pass it.

Harlo: Ritchey, Harlowton. Over.

Harlo: Ritchey, Harlowton. Over.
Harlo: Ritchey, Harlowton. Over.

The more they called, the madder and faster I got. I didn't answer them. Just kept on going. I turned and the fire had closed on me some more. I needed time when I got to the park to burn it. I pushed hard for the park.

I finally had to stop and leaned back against a tree. I raised my radio to call Harlowton, pushed the button, and said, "SOB!" I quickly released the button, but it went out over the air. "SOB!" I left my gloves when I tucked my pants in. Crap! Oh well, if I burn the park, I won't need them.

Me: Harlowton. Ritchey. (Each breath stabbed me in the chest).
Harlo: Ritchey. Harlowton. Go. Over.
Me: Park near. I have to "wag" and "dodge" it there. Over. (The dispatcher I was talking to, I had known for years. She didn't understand what I was really saying to her. Two things you were never to say over the radio: swear words and "I don't have fire gear." Our radios were monitored by lots of others, including the news media.)
Harlo: What? "Wag" and "dodge". Don't understand. Say again. Over.

Suddenly I heard—

GF: Harlowton. Break. Great Falls. Over.
GF: Ritchey. Great Falls. Over.
Me: Go Great Falls. Over.
GF: You said you have to "wag" and "dodge" at the *park*. Over.
Me: Ten-four. Over.
GF: Wag and dodge?
Me: Ten-four. Ever hear of that? Over. (I didn't know who I was talking to in Great Falls, but I knew he was a "head" of something.)

GF: Wag and dodge (pause). Is understood. How much wagging and dodging are you planning to do? Over.

Me: All of it! Over.

GF: What's your ETA to the park? Over.

Me: Don't know. Fifteen, twenty-five minutes? Over.

GF: Ritchey. Stand by.

Me: SOB! Now Great Falls was doing it to me!

GF: Ritchey. Great Falls.

Me: Ritchey. Go Great Falls. Over (I said, rather pissed off).

Gf: WD is a ten-four. The sooner the better. You equipped for it? Over.

Me: About 50 percent. Over.

About a minute pause from Great Falls. I knew they were cussing me.

GF: WD is still ten-four. Need ASAP fifteen or under. Can do? Over.

Me: Will give it 200 percent. Over.

GF: Call us at the park. Good luck. Over.

Me: Ten-four. Thanks. Over.

GF: Helio 1 is ninety out. Over.

Me: Ten-four. Ritchey out.

Thank God someone understood me. Now they knew I was going to back burn an area for safety and had given me the okay to do it. Although I would have done it anyway, they also knew I wasn't fully geared up—not good. Oh well, will worry about that if I get out of this mess.

I wish the "ninety out" for Helio 1 was ninety air miles and not the land one and a half hours I knew he meant. I had a slight hope of getting picked up by Helio 1 in the park, but it was too smoky for that.

The "wag and dodge" I had hoped someone would understand, was Wagner "Wag" Dodge. He was the crew chief of Smoke Jumpers, who jumped into the Mann Gulch fire north of Helena in August

1949. They didn't have the gear we have now—or really any gear. They had to run from the fire and in the last hundred feet to safety were trapped (see *Young Men and Fire* book).

Wag, knowing they were trapped, tried something. He lit a small area on fire. He convinced two of his crew to stay with him—the others went by him, refusing his order to stay. Only one hundred feet to safety. Wag and the two had to go through their new flames and laid down in the burnt grass to let the fire burn around and over them. The other thirteen were heading for safety (the last one hundred feet). The fire hit them all *hard, hot,* and *fast!* Wag and the other two in a small safety area that Wag lit, they lived. The other thirteen died within the last hundred feet! Everyone thinks they can make that last hundred feet. One hundred feet isn't far—except with fires. Wag was credited with doing the first safety burn—back burn.

Stone Mountain fire in Colorado in the '90s was similar to Mann Gulch fire. They lost crews there. All trying for that last hundred feet. Some of these were found feet from safety! A couple more steps, how could someone *not* make a few more feet? Easy, it's a *fire and when it slams you, you're dead in your tracks.* It's fast, unforgiving, and deadly. I lost two friends in the Stone Mountain fire.

My situation was a little better than either of these two, at least I hoped. I should have time to light the park and it would be a big safety zone. Every time I checked the fire, it was closing on me.

I finally reached the park and stood there horrified—the elk and deer hadn't been there to graze the grass down. The grass was about three feet high. At least it's super dry! It's going to burn really hot, but not as fast as I wanted it to. Too much fuel to bum up fast. I looked back—crap! The fire was about 150 yards behind, give or take. I would call Great Falls later, and I started lighting the edge of the park with my lighter. One thing about a Zippo, it usually lights the first time. It did! I lit about five spots, fifteen feet apart. I stepped back to watch it burn. Well, crap, it's burning but hardly moving west! I need a burned area to get into away from the timber. I checked behind me—a hundred yards away and closing. Getting hot here and smoky! I jumped over, around the back burn, and headed way out in the park. I started lighting more spots. I checked the timber fire—fifty yards and roaring. One of them has to burn and give me an area of burned-up grass for safety. I was now between two back burns.

This is going to be nasty! I had done all I could. I dropped to my knees. "Lord, I need a little help down here." It was all I could think of to say. I didn't know what else to do. The fires were burning, but not fast enough to give me a safety zone.

I saw the timber fire hit the grass and join the poorly started first back burn. I was standing there watching everything around me go up in flames, fast! The grass fire was coming at me like a speeding train now. I was going to run, but I saw my second back burn not doing much, so I turned and faced the fire. Watching it race toward you is hard to do! The grass fire appeared to be thirty feet high, but I am sure it was more like ten feet. I couldn't see over it or through it. It hit me—I had to go through it! Dodge said something about going through his.

I knew what was on the other side of the flames—burned-up grass that was now black ash dirt. No fire, no flames!

It was the whole width of the park now racing toward me. How deep it was, I didn't know. It couldn't be that far through the flames. I looked around; everything was on fire—the trees around the park had blown up, igniting the grass on all sides of me. Everything was racing to the center, burning up everything. It was all coming to me.

There comes a time in everyone's life when you know you have to bite the bullet. In one sense, it's a relief when you realize you have no other choice in the matter. Everything's settled now, the clock's running out. All you have to do is go through the motions.

My mind was made up—live or die! I had to go back through the flames.

I figured by the count of ten, I'd be through it. No, that's too long in flames! Count of five, I'd be through it. I took my helmet off and pulled out the earflaps. Button my shirt's top button, my sleeves down and tightened, I held my breath. "Protect my lungs, they can fix everything else" (USFS saying).

Shirt tail in. Hands and face? Hands and face? Cover my face with bare hands? This is going to be really nasty! 200 feet, 150 feet, 100 feet, this is it. My "last one hundred…fifty." I took off running right at it! Forty feet, thirty feet, twenty feet, ten feet. Held my breath, hands over my eyes, nose, and mouth. One…two…three…four…five…

I could hear my hands sizzling! It was too freaking hot. A breath at that moment was an instant killer. God, am I running with the flames or through them? I turned to the left some five…five…five, then I felt it, the temp dropped. I kept running then took a peek through my hands. Oh God, I made it through! I tried to slow down but must have cramped up. I went head over heels and ended up on my back. I was in black ash dirt—no fire, no flames! I was safe! It freaking worked! It worked! My hands tingled some not bad; I could handle that pain. Still on my back, I reached in my pocket and got my lighter, then a cigarette from my shirt pocket. I lit it and tried getting up. I couldn't, I was too weak. I lay there smoking my cigarette, nowhere to go anyway. I should call them (Great Falls) though. I reached for my radio in my belt case.

The radio was gone. Screw it; they know where I'm at! I finished my cigarette and flipped it away from me into the park and laughed. Nothing to burn here! I was pretty full of myself going back through a fire (now one of the very few to survive). It wasn't all that bad either. Burned the hair off my hands. Still just tingled some. I shut my eyes for a couple of seconds then opened them to make sure I had made it through. They know where I'm at. And shut my eyes again.

I woke later with a jolt. It felt like my cigarette fell on my cheek. I sat up and remembered I had thrown it away. Lord, that stings. Oh God, my hands were on fire, my neck was burning some. I couldn't get up. I rolled over and finally got up.

I remember just bits and pieces now and didn't know if they were true or not.

I walked for a while and found a puddle of water on a road of some sort. A pumper must have been here, I thought. I pushed my hands into the mud. Oh God, that felt good. I'm in heaven! What

relief! I smeared some on my face and neck. It was great! I'm staying here. Don't know how long I had been there, didn't even know where I was now.

Later I thought I saw some people—firefighters walking near me, but they would disappear if I looked directly at them. I could see timber, rocks, this road. When I tried focusing in on them, they vibrated. I didn't like that, so I just shut my eyes. I had to keep mudding up, my face, neck, and hands. It felt good! I noticed skin coming off my hands with the mud baths—didn't care. The mud felt great.

Suddenly, I felt a shaking of my shoulder and someone said, "Aw, Bob."

It sounded so pitiful. "Aw, Bob…" What the heck does that mean? I must have stood up because he was pulling, leading me. "You come with me. I'll get you cleaned up." When I opened my eyes, the whole world was spinning. I didn't like that feeling. I tried to sit up but felt hands all over me, pushing me back down.

Something was on my face and nose, but try as I did, I couldn't raise my hands.

Someone said, "Relax, you're okay." I was getting cold. I looked at my toes. "Where the heck are my clothes?"

Then I heard someone say, "Bob, you have to keep your hands in there."

"Where?"

Where the heck am I? Must have had my eyes closed. When I opened them, everything was blue. I heard someone say, "Fifteen minutes in, five minutes out." My hands started feeling great—the burning was leaving and my hands were cooling down. Then they started to get ice-freaking-cold! I tried moving them but couldn't. This was as bad as the burning!

I looked around, things still blue. I saw three or four people there around me. Sometimes I could hear them, other times their mouths moved, but I heard nothing.

The ice-cold feeling started to leave my hands—darn, they were feeling great again. I realized my hands were being held up in the air by people. I had a large tin bowl on my lap with a towel under it. The bowl had ice cubes and a brown liquid in it.

My hands started to burn again. I tried to put my hands in the bowl of ice. They wouldn't let me. The pain quickly became unbearable! Now I was yelling and swearing. Men don't scream, they yell. Someone said, "Fifteen minutes in, five minutes out." What the heck does that mean? I was trying to get away from the people holding my arms. My movement was restricted somehow. I couldn't move my legs except for an inch or two. Someone grabbed the ice bowl and took it. I was still yelling when the ice bowl returned. I came back to a moment of reality. I was in the hospital; the room was blue. I was strapped in a bed, part of which was up to keep me in a reclined position. I heard "Fifteen minutes in, five minutes out." My hands are getting ice-cold again. I tried to remove them, they held them in.

I was being tortured! I swore and yelled at them. They held on. I must have passed out. When I came to again, my hands were still in the ice. I suddenly ripped my hand out of the bowl, away from the one gal and swung at the other. I was so restricted body-wise, my swing missed by a mile. I passed out again.

When I woke again, my hands were just coming out and the gals were patting my arms with a towel, then quit and held them up. That was better. They were cold but warming up.

I realized I had something on my face—a wrap? My eyes, nose, and mouth were cut out. My hands were starting to burn again and I tried to ease them gently toward the bowl. They stopped me! "Fifteen minutes in and five minutes out." I begged, I swore, I yelled. They kept them from the ice. My hands were on fire!

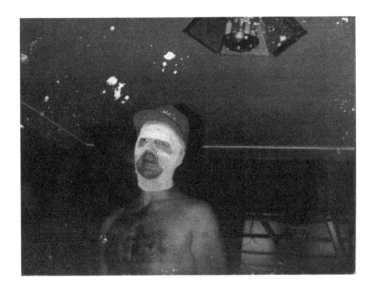

Finally, I felt the cooling of the ice—oh God!—and I was out again.

And so it went, my first night in the hospital. Pain and pleasure, pain and pleasure. It went on for hours and hours. It was more like pain-pain-pleasure-pain, then pain and pleasure.

When I came to, I could smell food and opened my eyes. A nurse with a food tray had come in.

Nurse: Would you like to eat something?
Me: Yeah!

I tried to sit up but couldn't seem to do it. She went to the side of the bed and cranked it up some.

Nurse: How's that?
Me: Great.

I asked her what happened. She just smiled.

Nurse: The doctor will be in shortly.

I looked at both my hands, both wrapped, very thickly wrapped. My fingers were spaced apart and wrapped separately. They tingled some, but it wasn't too much pain.

The nurse gave me a pill, a drink to wash it down with, and fed me. I had an IV in my left arm. She didn't say much as I ate. After I was done, we talked.

Me: Any chance of having a smoke?
Nurse: Don't think that's on your chart yet. (She laughed a little.)
Me: I'll buy you a car!

She smiled and shook her head no and pushed the cart to the door and stopped.

Nurse: What kind?
Me: What kind of what?
Nurse: Car! What kind of car?
Me: You look like a Boxster Porsche kind of person.
Nurse: Ha! And she left.

I knew I was in Harlowton Hospital. I was trying to remember the events of yesterday…if it had been yesterday. I was confused about everything. Then I remembered the bowl of ice! Lord, I couldn't stand anymore of that! Every once in a while, I'd see someone poke their head in the doorway.

Finally, a doc came in. I knew he wasn't one of the regular ones. He introduced himself, but his name was heard and forgotten. I remembered he said he was on loan here, a burn specialist from Canada.

He was checking the IV. I was really confused about what had happened. He interrupted my thoughts.

Doc: Well, you're doing great. How are you feeling this morning? Any pain?
Me: Doing good. What happened?

He explained I was on a fire and got burned.

Me: When? He smiled.
Doc: Yesterday sometime. You got here around seven thirty last
   night. Remember?
Me: I remember an ice bowl.
Doc: Yeah, that's pretty nasty, ah…(eh?)

I smiled at his "ah…" Canadians always put that at the end of
a sentence.

Me: What was the brown stuff in the bowl?
Doc: Benzedrine!

I moved my right hand toward my face.

Me: How bad?
Doc: Your face…a couple of spots…not that bad. I did that so the
   nurses would pamper you.

I held up my hands.

Me: How bad?
Doc: That's a different story. They got burned pretty good. I need to
   change the dressing, so let's take a look, ah?
Me: Yeah, I want to see them.

I was smiling about another "ah." I chuckled a little as I was
thinking, *God, I have to listen to "ahs" now, put me back in the ice bowl.*

Doc: When I take the wrap off your hands, it's going to sting a little
   when the air hits it. So be prepared for that, okay?
Me: Okay.

A nurse had come in with a cart of things for him to redo my hands, I guessed. He picked up a bottle and needle and filled the needle. I hate shots!

Me: What's that?
Doc: Morphine.
Me: Really? (I was surprised that they thought I needed it.)
Doc: You bet, good stuff. Will help you with the pain.
Me: I'll be okay. What's in the blue jar?
Doc: Silvadene. Really good for burns!
Me: Great.
Doc: Your hands are going to look bad to you, but don't worry. We can fix them…just not right away. Going to take some time.
Me: Like a skin graft?
Doc: No (pausing and thinking)… No, I don't think so. Let's see how things go, ah?

I smiled again at "ah."

Me: Yeah, okay, let's go.

He started unwrapping my right hand. He had a big wad of wrapping and a couple of layers to go. He cut the wad off and put it on the cart. He turned my hand over and cut up the palm and each finger. My hand was already tingling more.

Doc: This is going to sting a little. You ready?
Me: Sure, let's do it.

As he pulled the wraps off, the tingling increased immediately. He looked at me.

Doc: You okay?
Me: God, yeah! Hurry up!

My hand really started to burn again. Every second, the pain doubled. I can't handle this!

Doc: How you doing?
Me: Great! Hurry up!
Doc: Almost done. He quickly dressed and wrapped my hand. The Silvadene lowered the pain and the wrap brought it back to a tingle, manageable pain.
Doc: There, all done!

The lying jerk. "Going to sting a little." Why didn't he just say it's going to burn like heck? I wasn't ready for that! The pain made me forget to look at my hands. He moved some things on the cart.

Doc: Okay, ready to do the other one?
Me: Hell no. We can do it later!
Doc: Sorry! Need to do it now. How about that shot now? It'll relax you and ease the pain.

I was going to say no again, then I thought "screw macho!"

Me: Yeah, okay, give me a little.

So he gave me a shot and knocked me out. When I woke, I felt great, the hands were done and they were gone. Thank God!

I laid there for a while. This is boring! Now I had to pee. The sides of the bed were up, the IV was still in my arm, and my hands were wrapped thick! I pushed the light signal over to me, to call the nurse. Finally, I got it turned on by swearing at it. The nurse came in fairly quickly.

Nurse: Can I help you?
Me: Yeah, I need to go to the bathroom.

She grabbed a urinal jug and started toward me.

Me: My hands aren't working.
Nurse: I'll help.
Me: No, you'll help me to the bathroom!
Nurse: The urinal's easier.
Me: No, the bathroom.
Nurse: Number 1 or number 2?
Me: Really, I don't want to discuss this—the bathroom! Number 1!
Nurse: Okay.

She moved the IV around and lowered the side of the bed. She helped me sit up.

Nurse: Sit there for a minute.

I really, really had to pee now!

Me: Okay, let's go.

She finally got me and the IV to the bathroom.

Nurse: You okay now?
Me: Yeah, just leave.
Nurse: Okay, I'll be right outside the door.
Me: Great, shut the door!

She finally shut the door. There I stood with an IV in my arm on a pole, a robe split up the back, hands bandaged, and the toilet in front of me.

I had a hard time getting my robe up in front, then came the realization with these hands. This isn't going to work, I just couldn't figure this one out. I accidently said "shit" out loud.

Nurse: You okay?
Me: Yeah.

Nurse: Don't get pee on your hands. (Give me a break, woman. It wasn't working.)
Me: Nurse!
Nurse: Done already?
Me: No! (I said in a ticked-off tone.) I can't do this!

She opened the door.

Me: Can't do this with this robe and my hands like this.

She was trying to hold in a smile and probably a laugh.

Nurse: Why don't you sit down and pee?

I just stared at her for a minute. Crap! Didn't even think of that! Guys pee standing up, not sitting down. Must be the drugs! She shut the door again. I heard her snicker. God! As I sat there peeing, I looked at the toilet paper. Aw, crap! I held my hands out in front of me and looked at them. Crap! Crap! Another problem to be faced in the future. No way I could get toilet paper with these hands, let alone wipe my rear. I resolved I wouldn't do number 2 while in the hospital.

*****

The next morning, the doctor showed up again.

Doc: How are you doing this morning, Bob?
Me: Good, I guess.

The nurse came in with another cart. The doctor picked up a bottle and needle and started to fill it.

Me: What's going on?
Doc: Time to redo your hands.

Me: You got to be freaking kidding me. They're fine.
Doc: Sorry, need to do them again.
Me: I'm not going through *that* again!

He injected the needle in the IV. When I woke, they were gone and my hands redone.

Around noon, the crew stopped in to see me.

Joe: How you doing, Doc?
Me: How do I look like I'm doing? We all laughed.

Lori excused herself and left. I could tell she was upset a little about my burns.

Joe: Man, Doc, you went back through the fire?
Me: Yeah, guess I did. (Everyone was letting Joe ask their questions.)
Joe: So, what did it feel like?
Me: How does it look like it felt? (Everyone laughed.)
Me: Anyone got a couple of cigs and matches?

Al handed me two and a book of matches.

Me: Thanks.
Joe: Where you going to smoke them?
Me: Bathroom with the fan on. (Everyone laughed.)
Me: So the fire's out?
Joe: No!
Me: What are you doing here then?
Joe. They demob'd us that day.
Me: Really, why?
Joe: They thought you were dead.
Me: Oh yeah… (Guess they do that to a crew with a missing or dead member.)
Joe: Have us doing crap work over there now.
Me: Sorry!

Joe: Lots of talk about you with the chiefs.
Me: Good or bad?
Joe: Both really. They are ticked about no line gear though.
Me: Can imagine. Probably going to fire my ass as soon as I'm healed.
Joe: Don't think so.
Me: Really?
Joe: Bill said something about "killing that dumb ass." Ha-ha… (We all laughed.)
Joe: We got to get back.
Me: Thanks, guys!

They started to leave. Joe stopped at the door.

Joe: I heard Bill's coming over this afternoon.
Me: Great!
Joe: A "head" from Great Falls said you must have a hard time walking.
Me: Why?
Joe: 'Cause your balls must be this big!

He held his hands out wide. We both laughed and he left. Bill was head ranger at the compound and knew he was going to ream me.

At around three, Bill showed up and knocked on the door.

Bill: Hey, how you doing, Doc?
Me: Great, ready to go home and get back to work. (We laughed.)
Bill: Take your time, do what the doctor says.

Our whole conversation was just small talk. Bill finally stood up and walked to the door and stopped.

Bill: Hey, the fire's 80 percent contained now, have a good handle on it. Your back burn slowed it up pretty good.
Me: Great, glad I could help.

Bill kind of hung his head down and didn't say anything.

Bill: Did you really go back through the back burn?
Me: Yeah. Had to. Was my only chance.
Bill just looked at me for a few seconds.
Bill: Jesus, Doc!

He just shook his head and left. I heard him say another "Jesus" going down the hall.

*****

The next morning, the doctor and a nurse with a cart came in.

Me: You got to be freaking kidding me! (I was pissed.)
Me: You ain't doing that again… I can't handle it! It's too much!

He already had the needle ready and right into the IV. When I woke, my hands were all done and they were gone.
I pushed the signal button and the nurse came in.

Nurse: You okay?
Me: No, need the doctor!
Nurse: Pain?
Me: Need the doctor now!

I was faking a little pain for the nurse. I knew that if I told her I wanted to talk to him, it would be a while before he showed. Pain would bring him faster. Five minutes later, he showed.

Doc: Having pain, ah?
Me: No, I want to talk to you!
Doc: Okay. (He said, laughing some).
Me: How long do you think you're going to do that to my hands before I really get pissed?

Doc: Need to do it daily for a while.
Me: What? Like a week?
Doc: A little longer, I think.
Me: Little how long?
Doc: One or two—

I interrupted him.

Me: Two weeks? You're out of your mind, pal! Won't do it. Just shoot
    my rear, put an air bubble in that IV. This is too much! I—

He interrupted me.

Doc: Months!
Me: What?
Doc: Two months, maybe a little longer.
Me: You're freaking insane! I want out of here now. I'm done! Thanks
    for your help! You've been great!

Was trying to get the side down. He walked over to the IV. I
hadn't noticed there were two bags on the pole now. As he touched
it, I went out. I Woke up to the smell of food. *That jerk!* I thought.

Nurse: You have a visitor.
Me: Who?
Nurse: Bill.
Me: Thank God! Bring him in. (Bill entered.)
Bill: How you doing?
Me: Bill, I want the heck out of here today. Now get me the freaking
    release papers to sign.
Bill: Can't.
Me: What?
Bill: The Forest Service has to release you…not you. You're a federal
    employee.
Me: You're kidding me!

Bill: Nope, you're stuck here.
Me: I quit then!
Bill: Can't till you're released.

I just sat there, dead quiet, thinking, and really, *really* pissed off!

Bill: Great Falls will fly you to Seattle or Denver to a burn unit. Want to go?
Me: No, I can walk the fifteen miles home from here. Denver or Seattle would be an inconvenience for me to get home.
Bill: Good choice! He's a good doctor!
Me: I don't think I can handle this, Bill (tearing up a little). Don't think I can!
Bill: I'll talk to him and Great Falls and see if we can come up with something. Okay?
Me: Thanks, Bill.
Bill: You behave now!

Bill left, and I sat there thinking, *I'm losing it.* The nurse popped in.

Nurse: Ready to eat?
Me: Yeah!

*****

The next morning, the doctor and the nurse with another cart came in together.

Doc: How you doing this morning?
Me: Great! I said in a ticked-off tone.

He headed for the IV.

Me: Wait. Don't knock me out. I want to see my hands. I want to know what you're doing to them.

Doc: Going to be nasty. It will hurt a little, ah.

Me: Why do you say that? It's going to hurt like hell, just freaking say that, ah?

Doc: All right. (He smiled a little.) When I unwrap your hands and the air hits the raw meat, it's going to hurt like hell and I don't think you can handle it! I think you know you can't handle it!

Me: What do you mean *raw meat?*

Doc: Had to remove a lot of skin layers. You got burned bad. You got to accept that. You have about 16 percent burns. That's a lot! You're a medic, you know how bad that is. I'm hoping the layers will grow back without any problems.

Me: Okay, okay! Leave me awake for the first one and hold my hand up so I can see it—no matter what, okay? Then you can knock me out. I want to see it, though, okay?

Doc: Okay! Hang on! Here we go!

I made it to see my hand, then lights out. Wasn't good!

*****

I need to tell you about Lori:

Lori had actually saved my life the summer before. I'm one of those who are highly allergic to bee stings. I was also a medic for the State and the Forest Service. I gave each of my crew a sting kit to keep in their packs—just in case. I always had mine with me but never could give myself a shot. I had no problem giving one to someone else—Just not to myself. Every summer, I got stung and ended up in the ER.

On this day, I sent the crew a couple miles beyond, and Lori and I stayed behind to do a quick repair. A hornet flew up my shirt and stung me two inches from my spine. I needed to get to the ER in about fifteen minutes after getting stung. We were at least an hour away, on a rough mountain road. I couldn't drive fast, I was going to be "touch and go" getting to the ER.

I asked Lori if she had her sting kit. "God, you got stung again?" she asked.

"Yeah, sure did!"

She got her kit and the needle out. She asked me how it works. I told her to turn the "push" end till it stops. She did and was about to give me a shot in the arm.

"Wait," I said.

"You ever given shots before?"

"Sure, lots."

"Okay then."

She jammed the needle into my arm. Darn that hurt! After she gave me the first dose, I said, "Who'd you give shots to?"

"Horses, lots of horses," she replied.

"Let's go," I said.

And we took off. I told Lori to drive safely and sensible. "No wreck. Just get me out of the mountains. Once we hit the highway, then you can nail it."

I called the compound and told Barb I got stung again. She asked me our location and ETA. I told her "Castle Mountains and one hour."

I had been through this situation before with Barb. She knew fifteen minutes was the time I needed to be at the ER. She told me she would call the hospital and get the ambulance heading to us. The hospital being notified was okay, but I told her to forget the ambulance. It was a waste of time just to transfer me to it. Lori would bring me in. I told Barb we had two sting kits, plus tablets.

"I have four shots. Just took one, have three left. You should get me to the ER. I won't be in great shape though."

After slow driving on rough roads, we finally hit the highway. Barb had called the sheriff's department and a unit met us at the highway. I got my last shot there—wasn't feeling too good. The police unit led Lori in. I woke up in the hospital on my side with the local doctor giving me a shot at the sting site. I was there three hours before they let me go.

I wrote the incident up the next day and explained Lori's calmness and safe driving, shots, and other things. Lori was given a certificate of merit for bringing me in safely.

Eight days passed and every morning, I got through this ordeal. On the eighth day…

Doc: Bob, I have an idea that might work if you want to try it.
Me: What's that?
Doc: We might let you go home tomorrow. What do you think?
Me: I'm ready now.
Doc: No, tomorrow, with some restrictions.
Me: Like what?
Doc: You have to come to the clinic every morning. I think we could do this there, doing the new wraps. I'll let you be at home.
Me: Good idea! Yeah, I like it!
Doc: First time you skip it, you'll be back in here 'til you're healed—months!
Me: I won't skip. Promise.

I have never been back to that area since I got burned, although it's within driving distance of my home. I came close a couple of times but just couldn't go there. When asked why, I'd just say that I didn't want to find out that the past twenty years were actually the last few seconds of my life, and that I'm still at the fire. Then I usually try to laugh it off.

Memories can be as painful as the event sometimes. You find yourself asking God to let you have the day over again, or cursing yourself for not "doing this or that." "If only" becomes a part of your mental vocabulary. I guess I should be thankful that I survived "that day." Life is full of mistakes.

I was in the hospital eight more days before I was able to complain my way out. Every day I went through the new bandage thing. I still had to have it done daily for over a month as an outpatient. I would always stop at the Forest Service before, though, just to keep my presence there.

Bill asked me in his office one day for a talk. When I went in, it was small talk at first. Then he said, "Feel like talking about the fire?"

It wasn't really a question though. He said, "Great Falls staff wants to talk, when you want to. Someone from here will drive you up when you're up to it. Let me know when."

Then he started asking me questions, technical questions, and he was reading them off a couple sheets of paper in front of him. When I answered, he'd make some notes of my responses. Finally, he said, "Well I guess that's about it. Don't forget about Great Falls, okay?"

"Sure."

As I got to the door and had it halfway opened, Bill said, "How (pause) why did you go back through?" He wasn't sure if that should be a "how" or "why" question, or both.

I paused and said, "Two reasons, Bill. Two reasons."

I opened the door a little wider to leave and he quickly said, "What two reasons?" I leaned toward him and cupped my crotch with my mitten-sized wrapped hand.

"These two reasons."

He didn't smile, he didn't frown. I think my response indicated to him that I had the balls to do it, and that was why I did it; it caught him off guard.

Darn those pain pills! I shouldn't have done that to Bill, and I normally wouldn't have. If I got in trouble for saying and doing that, the pain pills made me do it. I was going to stick to that excuse!

Two days later, Moyra drove me to Great Falls for my meeting there. As we were driving, every once in a while, she'd kind of chuckle to herself. "Okay, what's the joke, Moyra?"

Finally, she said, between laughs and chuckles, "You might want to plead the Fifth when they ask you why you went through the fire." She laughed and laughed, and so did I.

"Can't believe Bill told you."

"He didn't. I was behind you when you did that. I didn't understand it at first. Larry explained it and then I understood."

We parked at the Great Falls compound and went in. I was offered coffee and a seat and told it wouldn't be long. Moyra went to visit some people she knew there. Some other people walked by and smiled and nodded at me. I nodded back. I still had my mask and hands wrapped.

After ten minutes, a lady came up to me with some papers. "Bob Ritchey?"

"Yes."

"Will you come with me?"

"Sure."

I was shown into a large room, five people in there. I didn't know any of them, but all had Forest Service uniforms on. Two women, three guys. *I'm screwed!* I thought. I was offered a seat; all had coffee, and I was offered some. I accepted. After a minute of small talk, one of the women said, "We want to ask you some questions about the fire and your injuries."

"Okay." All had papers and notepads in front of them. This was a bigger deal than I thought.

Question: #1: "Where was your fire gear?" (*Shit!* I thought)
Question #2: "Why didn't you have it on?"

I thought I had a great answer for that one. I wasn't going to fight the fire, only flag it. I've been on a lot of fires and seen the Heads on the fire. I quickly changed that to "seen the staff on the fire with fire clothes and a clipboard, no gear." I looked each one in their face as I said that. I was sure each had done it at one time or another. The reason was, they weren't fighting the fire. There's a time and place to do that—gear up. The mountain I was on was steep, and it was a hot day. I had a fire shelter in that pack—in fact, in all my four different packs. I had pulled it and gave it to a new AD for his line gear so he would have complete gear. (Actually, that was true, but that was the year before—didn't mention that part.) My line gear weighed 25 lbs, the max weight to have in it. The pack I took weighed 30 to 35 lbs. I didn't feel safe carrying both packs on that steep mountain.

For the next one and a half to two hours, with some breaks, I answered all their questions as best as I could. I explained my whole trip along with my thoughts, plans, and feelings. They were wrapping things up. The man in the center asked them if there were any more questions. I heard one of the women say quietly something like "Oh God."

I looked at him—he smiled and asked if I had any reasons for going back through the fire. I smiled right back and said, "I have a 'couple' of reasons.

(One of the women said, "Oh, God" under her breath, but a little louder.

"But everyone who is put in that position like I was will have their own reasons for going back through. A wife, a husband, children—the reasons are personal, and usually kept to oneself. My reasons wouldn't be yours and your reasons wouldn't be mine. It's something each one of us has to make for themselves." Both women still had their heads lowered some, but they were now looking at me just under their eyebrows.

"Your decisions involve many people. My decision only involved me; my crew was safe! I was doing what was expected of me. Harlowton didn't know they were sending me into a trap, and I didn't know I was walking into one. None of us even thought it was or could be a trap. If the call was called in an hour earlier, if better info on location had been given, if we'd found it earlier, I probably would've flagged the whole way around it. This meeting would never have occurred. You have to make your decisions from your standpoint. I had to make mine from my standpoint. I rely on you people to give me the best info and thoughts you have at the time, and you expect the same thing from me. I'd be in the ground right now and so would a lot of others if it wasn't for one thing—the training you provided to me and others. The thing that's really overlooked here is that you, the Forest Service, taught me to survive—not die. And so far, with me, you're batting 100 percent."

I was on a roll, giving them hell and saying all the right things, things they wanted to hear. I didn't have any of this prepared, it just came out.

"Thank you, Mr. Ritchey." And the meeting was over. Oops?

My hands were still being cleaned and wrapped daily by the Doc. My hands kept getting blacker and harder every day. The finger moved a little to a point, and then the "black crust" would crack or pull and cause pain. Every time they were unwrapped, the air caused intense pain. My face had healed great—had to look close to know where I got burned to even notice the spots.

My hands had a bad smell to them when unwrapped. One day, the Doc said, "I need to remove the back of your hands, the black crust. Your hands are doing great, and it's time to do it."

I said, "So when do you want to do it?"

Doc: "How about today, ah?"

"God, okay."

He called Diane, a nurse I knew—her husband was a rancher south of here. They talked a little by the door and she left. Doc and I talked a while about my hands. He said he had some good news. After removing the backs of my hands, maybe in a week or so, I wouldn't have to have them wrapped anymore. That didn't sit well with me! The pain when my hands were unwrapped was unbearable. But then I found out I would be wearing white wool gloves instead of the wrap. The gloves would be changed daily. Okay, that might work.

Diane came in the room pushing a cart with a bunch of stuff on it. I was sitting on a bed, the doc on a stool beside me. They talked a couple of seconds, then Diane started for the door. The doc asked, "Diane, you're not going to stay for this?"

"Nope," she said. "I've seen this before." She smiled at me and waved bye.

"This is going to hurt a little," the doc said. That meant it was going to hurt like hell! I was already hurting because the wrapping was off.

Me: Let's do it.
Doc: Want to lay down?
Me: No, I'm good.

He grabbed some long tweezers and surgical scissors. My hand was laying palm down on a towel on the cart. He carefully grabbed a piece of crust off the little finger on my left hand with the tweezers and snipped it with the scissors. My hand was already igniting again.

"Sh…" was all I got out. When I woke, I finished it, "…it!" My left hand was all done and wrapped. I had an IV in my arm and two nurses were with us now.

Doc: How you doing?
Me: Great! (I said in a little pissed-off tone)
Doc: Your hands are healing great—look really good. You're a good healer!

He turned slightly to the IV and was reaching for it when he asked if I wanted to stay awake for the other hand.

"N…" When I awoke, I finished it. "O." The right hand was all done. They sat me up and the nurses took the tray away. Doc said he was really pleased with the progress of the healing. The wrap wasn't the thicker wrap like before. My hands hurt, but it was a little different type of pain. It's hard to describe. They hurt, but the hurt felt kind of…good?

Doc reassured me that the hands were doing good. I asked about scarring. He didn't think there would be very much. He wanted me to make a fist with each hand as much as I could. I was going to do it, then I thought I'd be funny. So I asked if I was going to pass out again and started to laugh. He stopped me halfway through my laugh.
Doc: Fifty-fifty chance.
Me: What? Really?

He started laughing. "No, just do it slowly."

So, I did. I hadn't realized my fingers had basically been straight for over a month now because of the really thick wraps.

I slowly made a fist with the left. It was a little hard to do the first time, but it got easier each time I did it. I always did it slowly. My hands still hurt, but this pain felt…good? I tried explaining this "good pain" to him.

Doc: That's your body telling you that you're healing. It's a good sign!

It made me feel good. I made fists with the right. It seemed to be working okay. He told me to do it once or twice at a time, off and on during the day.

"You have some tendon damage from the heat in your fingers. It may work itself out, but we can fix them later if it doesn't."

I asked if he cut all the black off. He said he did, wrist to finger-nails, both hands. All ten fingers.

Doc: I'd like to ask you something, if you don't mind, Bob. I heard something about you the other day that I didn't know.
Me: Is it good or bad?
Doc: Don't think there's a good or bad to it. It might help me in treating burn patients.
Me: Go ahead, ask.
Doc: All I'd known was that you got burned in a fire. About a week ago, I heard you had gone back into the fire? How…why did you do it…go back into the fire? You had to know you'd be burned.
Me: That seems to be the question everyone wants me to answer. I haven't found the "great answer" to it yet. I guess I had to choose to live or die. I wasn't explaining it well, and he didn't understand.
Doc: Like suicide?
Me: No, I wasn't trying to commit suicide! I was trying to live! I found myself in a situation of a 99 percent chance of not living

through it. I had a 1 percent chance, though, of not dying. I guess I chose the 1 percent instead of accepting the 99 percent. I had a fire coming down on me fast in rough terrain. It was fast...and "slow" was my top speed. Time was running out. I was able to change the situation slightly, 1 percent, by moving. I found an area that might increase my 1 percent. So I set it on fire ahead of me.

Doc: What? The fire was burning behind you and you started a fire in front of you?

Me: Yeah, sounds dumb, right?

Doc: Guess I don't understand how this works. A fire behind you, so you start a fire in front of you to live?

Me: Actually, my first attempt to do it failed and I had to jump over it.

Doc: That's how you got burned?

Me: No, I moved again and started another fire in front of me.

Doc: So which fire did you get burned in? You have three fires burning now.

Me: The first one I lit is the one I had to go back through. When I said it failed, it only failed because of time. It didn't fail to burn. I had hoped it would burn up before the fire behind me caught up. The fire behind me was timber; the fire I lit was grass. The theory was, it would burn up and sort of burn out. Then I could go from the timber to a burned-out grassy area and be in safety. When the timber fire would get to this area, there would be nothing there to burn.

The timber fire came up too fast while lighting the first grass fire. I had to jump it—it wasn't burning very good yet. I went further in the grass and tried to do the same thing, hoping for more time. Then I was going to step into the burned area as it burned away from me. The timber fire hit the grass, and it was burning hot and fast toward me. The second fire I lit wasn't doing much of anything—no safe place to get to. I realized, as the grass was burning toward me, that the distance it had to go to get to me was creating what I needed:

a burned-up area with no fuel to keep it burning anymore. My only problem was to get to the burned-up area. I was on the wrong side.

Doc: You couldn't go around it?
Me: No. I was in the middle of a hundred acres of three-foot grass, surrounded by timber that was on fire, and it was setting all sides of the grass on fire.

Most people don't understand how fast a fire can move until they see it or experience it. I have seen it move in heavy timber half a mile or one mile in less than a minute, and that's being conservative. What happens is, it preheats ahead of the actual fire and "crowns." The tops of the trees ignite, which then ignite the tree tops near or ahead of it. It will move, ignite, faster than you could safely drive a vehicle through heavy timber. Once the top ignites, it burns down the tree. Temps on the ground under the trees kill any and everything very quickly. During the Yellowstone Park fire, an elk came out of the timber. The fire had burned the fur off of it. It ran past us forty feet and hit a tree head on. It just laid there. We went over and it was smoldering—dead and partly cooked. If elk, deer, and bears can't outrun a fire, how can a person? Your chances are very poor starting out. Doc, what do you think a lot of people do when they're surrounded by fire?

Doc: Don't know. What?
Me: They die! In California, some hid in their houses until they died. Some tried driving out and found out quickly that smoke comes in everywhere, even with the windows up. Faster if the A/C is on. In a vehicle, they're sitting on maybe twenty gallons of gas. One gallon of gas is equal to around five sticks of dynamite. It might be the other way around. It's nasty either way.
Me: I can't believe you chose to be a burn specialist. I couldn't deal with it every day. Dealing with my hands right now is tough enough. I can get dressed and drive, but that's about it. Can't zip or unzip my pants, can't get my shoes on or buckle my belt,

can't button my shirt. Had to sit to pee for a while and couldn't even wipe my rear. Pretty freaking humbling!

I'm glad you were here to treat me—that you're a burn specialist and not a GP. You're doing a great job, my only complaint is it's taking too long!
We both laughed.

Doc: Thanks for the insight on this. I never realized firefighters felt this way or see so much injuries. You should write it down, a book or lecture on it.
Me: Doc, the first thing I'm going to do when I get my hands back is forget this! Not write it down or talk about it.
Doc: You know what, Bob? I wouldn't want your job.
Me: Nor I, yours!

We laughed again.

Doc: See you tomorrow—make slow, easy fists.

I left.

*****

The next day, before going to the hospital to see Doc, I stopped at the Forest Service early. Bill saw me and said, "I was going to call you later"

Me: What about?
Bill: Two people are coming from Great Falls tomorrow. They want to talk to you again.
Me: Don't know what else I can tell them, Bill.
Bill: No, they want to talk to you this time.
Me: Gees, that doesn't sound good, does it?

I was hoping Bill would maybe give me some insight into about what. I was sure he knew more than he was saying.

Bill: Don't know, Doc. Basically said they needed to talk to you. Around ten o'clock?

I always liked it when Bill called me Doc—just made me feel good.

Me: Ten o'clock is fine. I'll be here.

We started to leave each other, then…

Me: Hey, Bill. (He turned back) You remember when you asked me what my two reasons were.

He started to chuckle and laughingly said, "Yeah!"

Me: I'm sorry about grabbing my crotch. I was taking pain pills and was a little silly on them. Hope I didn't offend you.

He laughed and said, "Doc, that was the best answer I ever got to any questions. Probably the most honest too. You had to have some balls to do what you did."

Me: Thanks, I guess.

We chuckled and parted company.

*****

I was dreading this meeting. I just knew I was going to get fired. I kept telling myself they can't, 'cause I'm still on medical leave. Maybe no more going to fires—that would hurt! I just couldn't figure it out. I was at the Forest Service at 0830. The "heads" showed up at 0900 and went straight to Bill's office. Around ten o'clock, they came out laughing a little. *That's a good sign!* They quit laughing when they saw me. Bill took us all downstairs to an office for our talk—rather "their" talk to me. I recognized both from Great Falls—one guy, one woman. The guy was the one who asked me "my reasons" and smiled at me. That was good…maybe?

The first couple of minutes was chitchat on how I was doing now, etc. Then it started out.

"You know you've caused us some real headaches," the woman said.

I remained silent but nodded a yes.

"We don't know what to do with you. In one sense, we like what you did—you used all your training and proved that it's good training, that it works, and that a firefighter can survive in a very dangerous and deadly situation. A lot of us still can't believe you did what you did. Some of us went to the fire area and tried to follow your exit path, as you told us. A tough, tough area. We went clear to the park. You know you set about 150 acres on fire?"

I halfway smiled and nodded yes, but remained silent.

"It would have burned anyway. Our best guess is you traveled about one and a half miles to get to the park. No easy feat, considering the fire was behind and below you. Jeff here was the one on the radio who understood your "wag and dodge" thing. He explained to us what you were going to do. Good Lord! What were you thinking?"

I started to say something, but she said, interrupting me, "That's not the question. We covered all that before!

You did everything right *except* (here it comes—the fire gear), the fire gear (almost smiled, then decided not to)! If you would have had the fire shelter with you, you realize you wouldn't have been burned at all."

I nodded yes.

She continued, "I called Moyra and had her pull all your packs out of the pumper. I asked her how many packs had fire shelters in them, except the one you had with you. You said you gave it to a new AD so he would have one for his gear. Right?"

"Correct," I said.

"Well, she did find three—one in each of your packs. I didn't think your med pack would have one, but it did. So I guess we will believe that you normally had one in the pack you lost at the fire— even though you gave it to someone else. I assume you didn't replace it because there wasn't enough here for all at the time?"

I nodded yes. *God, she's answering her own questions.*

"Nevertheless, that was your oversight on gearing up?"

I nodded again. "Probably everyone in Region 1 knows that a guy from District 0-6 went back through a fire and lived. Some think it was smart. Some think it was dumb. Some know you started another fire and some don't. Every time it's told, it gets crazier what you did. We have to put this all to rest somehow. We have ADs thinking they can start fires in a fire area now. Our training is screwed up unless we can correct this. There are only two answers to the problems you're causing for us. You know what they are?"

I nodded yes.

She said, "I'd like an answer to that."

Crap. Why did I say yes to that? So I said, "Fire my rear or…" *Crap, what would the second one be?*

So I said, "Forgive and forget?"

She said, "Forgive and forget? Forgive and forget? You've got to be kidding me! We have stories going around, and they keep getting crazier and crazier about what you did and how you did it."

(Since I had said, "forgive and forget," her volume level had increased a lot! I was sure they could hear her upstairs. I was getting reamed here.)

"It's like you're some super firefighter or something!" On and on, she went reaming me. "We decided what to do and we're all in 100 percent agreement on it."

God, here it comes.

"First, you are going to rewrite your whole fire story, top to bottom, and as honest an account as you can. The good, the bad, and the ugly of it.

"Second, after your story is given to Great Falls for approval and corrections, if any, you will give a talk at an R-1 meeting with most of R-1 there. That will be a day with most of the firefighters out of the field in the entire region." She sounded a little ticked!

"Third, at every orientation week for the new ADs, you will give a talk on fire gear, the use of and most importantly the keeping it all with you while on a fire. All of it! Got that?"

"Yes," I said meekly.

"After the talk on fire gear, you will tell your horror story with pictures, if you have some."

I nodded yes.

"You agree to this?"

"Yes." She paused, her back to me, then she turned and very nicely said, "Doc, you did everything right, but no shelter damn near got you killed."

She sounded almost concerned about me. She called me Doc. Wow! Bill must have told her my nickname.

"We want to show you a couple of things." Jeff reached under the desk and brought up a cardboard box he had carried down. He reached in and laid out something I didn't recognize. "Know what this is?" he asked.

I looked and said no.

"That is what is left of your $1500 Bendix radio you lost."

"Oops, sorry!"

She reached in and handed me an envelope. "Open it."

"Sorry," she said, looking at my gloves on my hands. She took out a sheet of paper and gave it to me. I opened it. It was an invoice for a hundred new fire shelters issued to D-6—almost sixty thousand dollars' worth! Wow!

Then she handed me a gift-wrapped box and undid the tape for me. It was heavy! I undid it carefully, as best as I could, and opened the box. I laughed. It was a brand-new fire shelter in a bright yellow Nomex (fire-proof) canvas carrying bag. On the case, in three-inch-high letters, was "DOC." When I saw this, I got something in my eye, which caused them to water, but I held it back…mostly. Apparently, they also got something in their eyes too.

We all got composed and were saying goodbye when she said, "One more thing. You can forget the 'two reasons why' part of your talk. That won't fly with a mixed group." We all laughed at that.

Jeff stuck out his hand to shake mine, then realized that wasn't going to work. He gave me a pat on the shoulder and said, "Another time and get healed."

Gloria gave me a peck on the cheek, which surprised me.

They went upstairs and I stayed downstairs for a while. When I finally went upstairs, everybody there looked at me and said, "Forgive and forget?" We all laughed.

So I ended up writing my little horror story and telling it once or twice every fire season. Since retiring, I don't tell the story and no one asks. I shoved it in the memory files. I don't pull it out often. Most of those who were around then are retired and moved on now.

For a long time after my burns, many things were answered by, "Well, I have two reasons for doing this or that. Everything had two reasons! Even some of the gals started saying, 'I've got two reasons too for…'"

It was a good time being in the Forest Service.

R-1 and D-6. I loved it!

My hands healed and only one finger has a tendon problem. I still live with pain in the hands. It gets triggered when the water or air is too cold or too hot. I put a pair of gloves on, and it seems to go away. I went to a doctor one time and he said, "You know that pain is in your head now, not your hands." Either way, it still hurts like heck.

Sometimes, when I'm walking through a fire camp, I heard someone say to another, "See that guy (me)? He went back through a forest fire and got burned." A legend in your own mind, Ritchey.

The best one was while I was eating on a fire in the mess tent. The guy beside me poked me and said, "See that big guy over there?"

"Yeah."

"He went through a big-ass fire and got burned really bad."

"Wow, unreal! I couldn't do that. Could you?"

"No way, man. No way."

I heard my story told a lot of different ways. The story was living on in a distorted way and some big muscular guy, eighteen to twenty years old, was getting pointed out. The one who did it—six years earlier!

Aw, heck, maybe that guy did keep going into a fire and carrying his crew out one by one while he was on fire.

Me? I was just damn lucky to get myself out, singed a little around the edges.

ABOUT THE AUTHOR

Robert "Bob" Ritchey was born on April 1, 1949, and passed away on September 27, 2019, at the age of seventy years old. He enjoyed music, playing both acoustic and electric guitars. He loved the outdoors, planting a garden every spring and fishing all year long and hunting in the fall. He never married but enjoyed my kids and grandkids, teaching them to shoot bows and arrows and .22 rifles. He spent most of his life having people trying to "April fool" him every year. He spent two years at Moorhead State University, taking basic classes. Then he decided he would be an "honest" car salesman. He did well in that occupation in Pennsylvania, Montana, and Colorado, but it seemed that was not quite enough. So he moved to Shawmut, Montana, buying property next to our parents. He went to work for the Lewis & Clark Forest Service in Harlowton as a wildland firefighter and EMT. As he worked in the forest service, he discovered this was his niche in life where God wanted him. With our dad being a preacher of God's word, we learned to put God first, family second, and job and everything else third. Bob learned to do all three in the forest service. He was working in God's country, the firefighters became his family, and he loved being able to help by fighting fires. His family is proud of him.

Printed in the USA
CPSIA information can be obtained
at www.ICGtesting.com
LVHW061437210124
769497LV00043B/1473